Rap it up

QUESTIONS

PUBLISHING
COMPANY

Rap it up

reading, writing & performing

rap poems in the classroom

Compiled by James Carter

Illustrated by Jilly Wilkinson

The Questions Publishing Company Ltd,
Birmingham
2000

First published in 2000 by
The *Questions* Publishing Company Ltd
27 Frederick Street, Birmingham B1 3HH

Design by Al Stewart
Illustrations by Jilly Wilkinson
Cover design by Al Stewart, illustration by Jilly Wilkinson

ISBN: 1-84190-043-5

Also available from Questions Publishing Company Ltd:

Jenny Kissed Me: an anthology of poems about love, with teaching resources for KS2
Compiled by Fred Sedgwick
ISBN: 1-84190-036-2

The Key Stage 2 Poetry Pack
Alan Peat
ISBN: 1-84190-044-3

Questions Literacy Resources

The Story of Tracy Beaker based on the story by Jacqueline Wilson and compiled by Liz Ross
ISBN: 1-898149-82-8

Bill's New Frock based on the story by Anne Fine and compiled by Marian Dean
ISBN: 1-84190-030-3

Contents

ACCOMPANYING CD

1. Valerie Bloom – 'Mega Star Rap'
2. Valerie Bloom – 'Haircut Rap'
3. Brian Moses – 'Clapping Rap'
4. Brian Moses – 'Mobile Phone Rap'
5. Instrumental Rapping Track #1 (slow tempo)
6. Instrumental Rapping Track #2 (medium tempo)
7. Instrumental Rapping Track #3 (medium tempo)
8. Bonus Instrumental Track – 'Rap It Up'

Valerie Bloom and Brian Moses perform their own poems on the CD; these also feature in the anthology section of this book.

The three instrumental rapping tracks and bonus track 'Rap it up' composed by James Carter, produced and recorded by Mark Hawkins and James Carter. The CD is a Stereo Architects of Sound production.

For Molly, with all my love

Acknowledgements

Acknowledgements are due to the following copyright holders:

Valerie Bloom for 'Haircut Rap' and 'Mega Star Rap', from *Rap With Rosen*, Longman.

James Carter for 'The Charles Darwin Rap', previously published in *Hysterical Historicals: The Victorians*, anthology chosen by Brian Moses, Macmillan; and also for 'Cool or Cruel', 'I'm Watching You', 'Puss-in-Footie-Boots', 'Shaggy Dog Rap' and 'Madcap Rap', all published here for the first time.

Paul Cookson for 'Santa's Christmas Rapping Caper', published here for the first time.

Gina Douthwaite for 'Tell-Tale Rap', from *Doin' Mi 'Ed In*, an anthology chosen by David Orme and Martin Glynn, Macmillan. © Gina Douthwaite, 1993.

John Foster for 'The Schoolkids' Rap', published here for the first time.

Andrew Fusek Peters for 'The Moon is on the Microphone', from *The Moon is on the Microphone* by Andrew Fusek Peters, Sherbourne Publications.

Jack Ouseby for 'Gran Can You Rap?', from *Unzip Your Lips: 100 Poems to Perform*, chosen by Paul Cookson, Macmillan.

Tony Mitton for 'Little Red Rap', from *Big Bad Raps*, by Tony Mitton, first published by Orchard Books in 1996, a division of The Watts Publishing Group Limited, 96 Leonard Street, London EC2A 4XD; and also for 'The Write a Rap Rap', previously published by Heinemann in the Literacy World Series, reproduced by permission of Heinemann Educational Publishers, a division of Reed Educational and Professional Publishers Limited.

Wes Magee for 'Doin' the Rhythm of the Boneyard Rap', published here for the first time.

Yvonne Mitto for 'Teenage Meanage', previously published in *Doin' Mi 'Ed In*, an anthology chosen by David Orme and Martin Glynn, Macmillan. © Yvonne Mitto, 1993.

Brian Moses for 'Clapping Rap' from *Croc City*, published by Victoria Press, and 'Mobile Phone Rap' published here for the first time.

Grace Nichols for 'Baby-K Rap Rhyme', from *No Hickory No Dickory No Dock*, by Grace Nichols. © Grace Nichols 1991, reproduced by permission of Curtis Brown Ltd., London.

Chris Riley for 'September Shoe Rap', reproduced from *Unzip Your Lips: 100 Poems to Perform*, chosen by Paul Cookson, by permission of Macmillan Children's Books, London.

Norman Silver for 'New World Dream Rap', published here for the first time.

Benjamin Zephaniah for ' I De Rap Guy', from *Funky Chickens* by Benjamin Zephaniah, Viking 1996. © Benjamin Zephaniah, 1996.

Other poems/books cited:

'RAPunzel' by Patience Agbabi, can be found in *Doin' Mi 'Ed In*, an anthology chosen by David Orme and Martin Glynn, published by Macmillan.

Alice in Wonderland by Lewis Carroll, is published by Penguin Classics.

'The Walrus and the Carpenter' and 'A-sitting on a Gate', come from *Alice Through the Looking Glass*, by Lewis Carroll, published by Penguin Classics.

The Demon Headteacher by Gillian Cross is published by OUP/Puffin.

James and the Giant Peach and *The Fantastic Mr Fox* by Roald Dahl, are published by Puffin.

The Iron Man by Ted Hughes is published by Faber & Faber.

Tony Mitton's collections of rap poems, including *Big Bad Raps*, *Royal Raps*, *Monster Raps* and *Fangtastic Raps* are published by Orchard Books.

'Down Behind the Dustbin' by Michael Rosen can be found in *You Tell Me* by Michael Rosen and Roger McGough, published by Puffin.

'The Michael Rosen Rap', by Michael Rosen, appears in *The Hypnotiser* by Michael Rosen, published by Scholastic Press.

Harry Potter and the Philosopher's Stone by J K Rowling is published by Bloomsbury.

The majority of Jacqueline Wilson's novels are published by Transworld.

Goosebumps and *Point Horror* are imprints of the Scholastic Press Ltd.

The animated feature films *Toy Story* (1996), *Toy Story 2* (2000), *A Bug's Life* (1999) are Disney productions, directed by John Lasseter of Pixar; *The Jungle Book* (1967) is a Disney production, directed by Wolfgang Reitherman.

Very special thanks to the following for their wonderful raps: Laurence and Alasdair Fitz-Desorgher; Megan Campbell; Andrew Reid's Year 6 class at Bangabandhu School, Bethnal Green in London for 'Bethnal Green Rap' – written during a rap workshop run by Valerie Bloom.

Extracts from interviews with Tony Mitton, Benjamin Zephaniah, Valerie Bloom, John Foster, Brian Moses and Gaby Morgan are reproduced with permission.

Introduction: Why rap?

Indeed, why rap? Why should we entertain and promote rap in the classroom? Well, there are a number of good reasons. First, it is a contemporary genre, popular with young people. Not only is rap fun but it has much to offer as an educational tool. It is an excellent model for reading, for discussion and for analytical work, as well as for practical activities such as creative writing and performing. Rap also acts as a perfect forum in which to explore key poetic devices such as rhythm, rhyme, alliteration, assonance and narration.

On top of all this, rap is a form that will allow children to use their own voices and their everyday language, to write as they speak, with their own dialects. As a result, some of those children who do not usually take to poetry – and in particular, such aspects as metaphor and figurative language – may well enjoy rap. And perhaps an interest in rap might in turn lead to an appreciation of some of the other forms of poetry.

Rap has a long history, with its origins in toasting – rhythmical talking – to reggae music, and further back to the African griots – musicians-cum-poets-cum-storytellers. But rap, in the form that we know it now, began in the 1970s, as part of the New York underground hip hop movement.

Rap poetry – the literary offshoot of rap – has been growing in popularity since the 1980s and has become a respected poetic and cultural form (a far cry from gangsta rap and hardcore hip hop) – one that is recognised by both the National Literacy Strategy and the National Curriculum. Similar to rap poetry is an African-Caribbean form known as 'dub poetry', which is also very much part of the oral tradition. Like rap, it places emphasis on rhythm and rhyme. Current exponents of dub poetry include Linton Kwesi Johnson and Benjamin Zephaniah.

But really, rap is not so much a medium or a genre, it is more a form of communication, a means of self-expression, effective for telling stories, spreading messages or conveying our feelings to the world around us. Nowadays, rap is a pan media phenomenon – to be found in films, television programmes, cinema and television adverts, cartoons and radio jingles in languages and cultures across the globe.

Rap it up is divided into three parts :

    ☆ ANTHOLOGY of rap poems

☆ TEACHERS' MANUAL with advice and ideas for reading, writing and performing raps (includes photocopy sheets and workshops)
☆ COMPACT DISC

The ANTHOLOGY has been compiled to provide classes with rap poems from a variety of current and respected children's poets, including Valerie Bloom, Benjamin Zephaniah, Tony Mitton, Grace Nichols, Brian Moses and John Foster. The raps represent a range of voices, tones and subject areas, and many of them have been performed with great success in schools.

The TEACHERS' MANUAL with its related workshops seeks to provide contexts and opportunities in which children can :

☆ use rap poems by professional poets as models
☆ consider both the form and content of rap poetry
☆ practise aspects of the creative process – including brainstorming, improvising and re-drafting
☆ explore a variety of poetic and literary elements such as rhythm, rhyme, narrative, narration, alliteration and assonance
☆ create synonyms – words and phrases
☆ develop performance and accompaniment skills

The COMPACT DISC features two poets, Valerie Bloom and Brian Moses, performing their own rap poems. In addition, the CD contains three musical backing tracks that children can perform, write or even improvise rap poems to.

On a personal note, I would like to thank a great many people and to say that this book has been much fun to produce. It is the third book with which I have had the pleasure and privilege to work with editor Helen Fairlie, who has been as warmly supportive, adventurous and imaginative as ever. Helen – many, many thanks once again. Thanks also to illustrator Jilly Wilkinson for her commitment to this project and for her wonderful artwork in the anthology section.

Thanks also to my musical partner Mark Hawkins – a professional composer and musical alchemist – for putting in so many hours and for helping me to assemble the music for the CD. Thanks must also go to my wife Sarah for her impeccable home editorial service. Thanks to Ian Brown for his poetry and footie expertise. Thanks too to David Wilkinson for his perpetual philanthropy.

I wish to thank Megan Campbell and Laurence and Alasdair Fitz-Desorgher for the many enjoyable hours we have had writing raps together. Thanks to Andrew Reid and his Year 6 class at the Bangabandhu School for allowing me to observe Valerie Bloom's rap workshop that resulted in the wonderful poem 'Bethnal Green Rap' which is featured in the teachers' manual of this book.

Thanks to Brian Moses and Valerie Bloom for taking time out of their busy schedules to record their raps. Further thanks must go to Brian Moses for allowing Mark Hawkins and me to convert his study into a recording studio for the day.

The publishers and I would very much welcome any feedback or responses that teachers may have to the material in this book/CD. We hope that *Rap it up* will prove to be an enjoyable and valuable resource.

James Carter
Autumn 2000

Anthology of rap poems

Anthology Contents

Little Red Rap

Tony Mitton

Just on the edge of a deep, dark wood
lived a girl called Little Red Riding Hood.
Her grandmother lived not far away,
so Red went to pay her a visit one day.

She took some cake and she took some wine
packed up in a basket nice and fine.
And her ma said, 'Red, now just watch out,
for they say that Big Bad Wolf's about.'

But Red went off with a hop and a skip.
She was feeling good, she was feeling hip.
So she took her time, she picked some flowers,
and soon the minutes had grown to hours.

And the Big Bad Wolf who knew her plan,
he turned his nose and he ran and ran.
He ran till he came to her grandmother's door.
Then he locked her up with a great big roar.

He took her place in her nice warm bed,
And he waited there for Little Miss Red.
So when Little Red she stepped inside,
that wolf, his eyes went open wide.

Says Red, 'Why, Gran, what great big eyes!'
Says Wolf, 'I'm trying you out for size,'
Says Red, 'Why, Gran, you're covered in hair!'
Says Wolf, 'Now, dear, it's rude to stare.'

Says Red, 'Why, Gran, what great big claws,
what great big teeth, what great big jaws!
And goodness, Gran, what a great big grin!'
Says Wolf, 'All the better to fit you in!'

But Little Miss Red says, 'Not so fast . . .'
And she calls to a woodcutter strolling past.
'Hey, you there, John! Can I borrow your axe?'
And she gave that Wolfie three good whacks.

'That's one from Gran and one from me
and one delivered entirely free.'
That wolf ran off with a holler and a shout
and Little Miss Red let Grandma out.

They called the woodcutter in to dine
And they all sat down to the cake and the wine.
And that's how the story ends . . .
Just fine!

Cool or Cruel? (Wol's Rap)

James Carter

We've all heard tales of wolves like me
Telling what bad guys we're meant to be
Now I wouldn't say they're a pack of lies
But listen up close – you'll soon get wise

My name is Wol – I'm neat, I'm cool
Unlike my dad, who's mean and cruel
Now how'd you like to be the son –
Of the Big Bad Wolf ? No, it ain't much fun –
As everyone thinks I'm just like him
But I don't scare folks – it ain't my thing
Wherever I go, as you will see
People always yell at me:

Hey wolfie –
Get out of town!
We don't want guys like you around
You gobble up grans, you puff little pigs
We've all had enough of your lies and tricks!

Now here's the thing to change your mind
on hip little Wol and his wolfie kind
So gather up close, take a seat, relax
and check these out – my radical raps

Out for a walk in the woods one day
Cruisin along, I'm makin' my way
I meet young Gretel and Hansel too
Chewing on a house – what a thing to do!
I say, 'Hi dudes, hi! Gimme high five!
Fancy a stroll with hip little Wol?'
What d'ya think will happen next?
They yell at me, as you might've guessed:

Hey wolfie –
Get out of town! . . .

They don't want to hear my hip-hop tune
So I take to the path and then very soon
I meet a princess, she's kissin' this frog
I don't know 'bout you, but I think that's odd!
I say, 'Hi dudes, hi! Gimme high five!
Fancy a stroll with hip little Wol?'
What d'ya think will happen next?
They yell at me, as you might've guessed:

Hey wolfie –
Get out of town! . . .

They don't want to hear my hip-hop tune
So I take to the path and then very soon
Seven little dwarfs come marching along
'Hi-Ho Hi-Ho' – what a funny old song!
I say, 'Hi dudes, hi! Gimme LOW five!
Fancy a stroll with hip little Wol?'
What d'ya think will happen next?
They yell at me, as you might've guessed:

Hey wolfie –
Get out of town! . . .

They don't want to hear my hip-hop tune
So I take to the path and then very soon
I see Cinderella in just one shoe –
Is that a fashionable thing to do?
I say, 'Hi babe, hi! Gimme high five!
Fancy a stroll with hip little Wol?'
What d'ya think will happen next?
She yells at me, as you might've guessed:

Hey wolfie –
Get out of town! . . .

She doesn't want to hear my hip-hop tune
So I take to the path and then very soon
A mighty big granny jumps out a shrub
With a basket full of tasty grub
She's a hairy chin-chin and mighty big feet
And big sharp claws and mighty sharp teeth
But this great big gran looks kind of wrong
But still I sing my hip-hop song:
'Hi babe, hi! Gimme VERY HIGH five!
Fancy a stroll with hip little Wol?'
What d'ya think will happen next?
Does she yell at me, as you might've guessed?

Hey wolfie –
Get out of town! . . .

NO WAY!
This big old weird old biddy old gran
Rips off her clothes – and it's my old man:
The Big Bad Wolf – he was in disguise
And there he stands, before my eyes!
And then Dad howls, 'Wol, listen to me!
You're letting down the family
We've all had enough of you being so cool
Now get out get there and be real *CRUEL*!!

So I say 'COOL!' And he says 'CRUEL!'

And I say 'COOL!'

and he says 'CRUEL!'

Then just as this is going down
the fairy tale folks all gather round –
Hansel, Gretel and Cinderella
The princess, frog, the little fellas
And what d'ya think that they might say –

Hey wolfies –
Get out of town! . . .

NO WAY!:

Hey wolfies –
What'ya gonna do?
What'ya gonna be now – cool or cruel?
D'ya gobble up grans or help 'em out?
D'ya puff little pigs or build 'em a house?
So sort it, right? Then give us a shout!

So Dad and I we talk it through
At last we find what's best to do –
Dear readers, we'll let YOU decide
We'll let you make up your minds
The vote is yours, it's up to you
Are we WICKED or *WICKED* – COOL or *CRUEL*?
Your answers on a postcard please
To: Little Wol's House by the shady trees
Or if e-mail, you can buzz it along
To the 3 w's.Wol.com
Please write it now and don't delay
We'd love to know what you've got to say

My rap is done – so I'll wrap it up now
This Wol's gonna stroll – chill out, ciao!

Dodo Rap

Ian Beck
(excerpted from Jack and the Dodo, a musical entertainment for children by Ian Beck and Glynn Boyd Harte.)

The dodo is an extinct bird that once lived on the island of Mauritius in the Indian Ocean. The dodo was flightless and built its nest on the ground. It was discovered by the Portuguese when they colonised Mauritius in 1598. The dodo was hunted by the colonists as well as the animals that were imported onto the island. As a result, the dodo was extinct by 1681. The word 'dodo' is Portuguese and means 'simpleton'.

'Dodo Rap' rap comes from a musical. At this point in the story, the poor Dodo has been caught at the express wish of a collector who needs just one dodo to complete his set of endangered species. The Dodo is in a cage and raps this lament:

Here I am, an' I'm a Dodo bird
And just in case you think I'm absurd
I can tell you now I'm a dude distinct
And I'm standing here on the edge of the brink
Seconds away from the land of extinct

I'm standing chained on the edge of the brink
My flock all gone, on the brink of extinct
An' I'm filled with woe, an' I'm gonna die
An' I'm gonna die, 'cause I just can't fly
Then they'll get their fill of their death wish thrills
When they kill me – when they kill me

Such is the truth of the way of men
Why they locked me up in this little pen
I'm a D,D,D
I'm an O,O,O
I'm a D,O, D,O Dodo do.
Oh no!

There once was a time I had a little sister
And all that time I never knew I'd miss her
And there was a time I had a brother too
You know what they did? They turned 'em into stew

Well that's not all, if you think that's rough
They ate my granny, though she was rather tough
Then they fried up all of my poor old cousins
Fried 'em up slow in batches of dozens
Then they cut up all my lovely little nieces
Into lots and lots of tiny weeny pieces

Such is the truth of the way of men . . .

And I'm gonna cry, yes I'm gonna cry
When push comes to shove, I don't wanna die
'Cause I'm a dude of distinction
I'm risking my extinction
I'm a Dodo do with attitude
And pardon *me* if you think *I'm* rude
But if you was locked up in this cage
Perhaps you'd get in a mighty rage

'Cause it's mankind that chased us
And almost erased us
It's their way of hate put our lives on a plate
It's the way of man flushed us down the pan

Such is the truth of the way of men . . .

The Charles Darwin Rap

(or The Dodo's a No-no)
James Carter

In 1831 Charles Darwin travelled on a ship called 'The Beagle' to study plants on the islands in the Atlantic Ocean. But he did much more than study plants – he began to think about how all living things: plants, birds and animals, came to be how they are now. When he returned home to England, he began work on a book called *On the Origin of Species*. In this book he wrote about many things, including 'evolution' – that is, the way animals developed and evolved over millions of years. Darwin also talked about the possible reasons why some types of animals have survived, and others, such as the dodo bird, haven't. He called this idea 'the survival of the fittest'. Rather than print out the whole book for you, here's a mini-version, rap-style. Take it away, Mr Darwin:

I've been over the seas, now I'm back to stay
To tell you some stuff that'll blow you away
It's a whole new thing I've been thinking about
Gonna rattle your cage before I'm out

I'm not so sure about Adam and Eve
And you'll find this really hard to believe
That I see the world as a family tree
Going way, way back into history

As I believe we're related to apes
For aren't we both called 'primates'?
And apes are related to lions and cats
And they're related to the birds and the bats
And they're related to lizards and snakes
And they once came from frogs in lakes
And frogs were fish, who were micro-dots
And before that – well, who knows what?!?

It's radical – not magical – historical – not tragical
It's logical – biological – theological – philosophical

Evolution – my philosophy
Evolution – how we came to be
Evolution – it's my world view
Evolution – d'you believe it too?

You may think it's *wicked*, man
to say we come from Orang-Utans
and an ape is our great-great-great-great-great-great-great-gran!

And that's not all, I've another idea
'bout why some things are no longer here
Well, you got to be fit if you wanna survive
If you're not, well, it's bye-bye!

Survival – you got to be tough
Survival – or is it luck?
Survival – it's a way of life
Survival – if you want to survive

The dodo's a no-no – the donkey's a go-go
Why did one live – and the other die?
You gotta be fit if you want to survive!
And what do *you* think – am I right?!?

New World Dream Rap
Norman Silver

Can you hear the celebration
spreading all around the nation?
Like a flaming supernova
love is breaking out all over.

Do you see the warning
written on the sky?
Come another morning
it may be you or I.

Screams of joy and jubilation
reach across the whole creation.
From Shanghai to the Cliffs of Dover
love is breaking out all over.

Is it so outrageous
to love your fellow man?
Love is so contagious,
catch it if you can!

Say good bye to desolation
there will be no more starvation.
Like a field of four-leaf clover –
love is breaking out all over.

Can you hear the beating
of the marching drum?
No use now retreating
your glory day has come.

When the final transformation
starts to shake the old foundation,
it will be a giant pushover –
love is breaking out all over.

What have you been dreaming?
Is it so absurd
to find a hidden meaning
in the freedom of a bird?

When the train calls at your station
jump aboard – no reservation.
Like a travelling Gypsy Rover,
love is breaking out all over.

Can you hear the ringing
of the golden bell?
A silent voice is singing:
'Old world fare thee well!'

Baby-K Rap Rhyme

Grace Nichols

My name is Baby-K
An dis is my rhyme
Sit back folks
While I rap my mind;

Ah rocking with my homegirl;
My Mommy
Ah rocking with my homeboy,
My Daddy
My big sister, Les an
My Granny,
Hey dere people – my posse
I'm the business
The ruler of the nursery

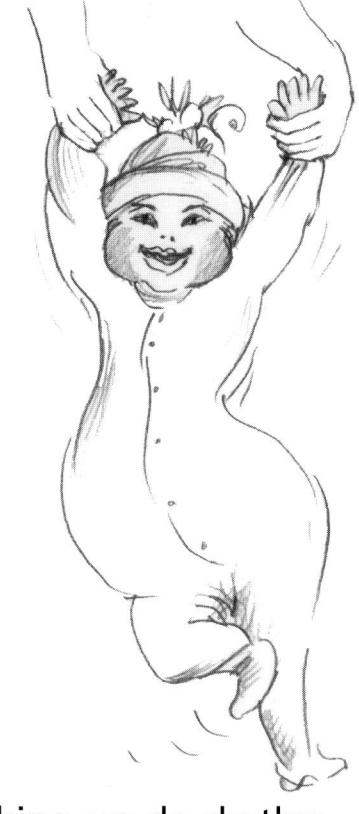

poop po-doop
poop-poop po-doop
poop po-doop
poop-poop po-doop

Well, ah soaking up de rhythm
Ah drinking up my tea
Ah bouncing an ah rocking
On my Mommy knee
So happy man so happy

poop po-doop
poop-poop po-doop
poop po-doop
poop-poop po-doop

Wish my rhyme wasn't hard
Wish my rhyme wasn't rough
But sometimes, people
You got to be tough

Cause dey pumping up de chickens
Dey stumping down de trees
Dey messing up de ozones
Dey messing up de seas

Baby-K say stop dis –
please, please, please

poop po-doop
poop-poop po-doop
poop po-doop
poop-poop po-doop

Now am splashing in de bath
With my rubber duck
Who don't like dis rhyme
Kiss my baby-foot
Babies everywhere
Join a Babyhood

Cause dey hotting up de globe, man
Dey hitting down de seals
Dey killing of de ellyies
For dere ivories
Baby-K say stop dis –
please, please, please

poop po-doop
poop-poop po-doop
poop po-doop
poop-poop po-doop

Dis is my Baby-K rap
But it's a kinda plea
what kinda world
Dey going to leave fuh me?
What kinda world
Dey going to leave fuh me?
 Poop po-doop.

I De Rap Guy

Benjamin Zephaniah

I am de rapping rasta
I rap de lyrics fasta
Dan a Ford Cortina
Or a double ghetto blasta,
When royals are listening
They proclaim me as a king
I am way out an travelling
Not a puppet on a string.

I am de rapping rasta
De lyrical masta
Dey say I am good to go
So I go wid de flow,
If yu really want to know
Yu should book me for a show
I will tek yu high an low
Like an eagle or a roe.

What I spread is unity
Or to put it simply
I want racial harmony
In de world community,
I am big an I am bad
So bad I will mek you glad
An you'll hav to tell ya Dad
Bout de rapper yu just had.

I rap on de move
Wid a little tongue an groove
Wid ability to soothe
Warmongers may not approve,
I can put yu in your place
Wid a little drum an bass
I am proud of every race
I out ran de steeplechase.

I am de rapping rasta
Flesh an bone not plaster
My ideas are very green
An I keep me rapping clean,
Let me take you on a tour
I know what I'm rapping for,
I can rap from coast to coast
an I don't like to brag or boast.

I'm Watching You

James Carter

Now I'm not stupid – I'm no fool
I know what's happening in your school
I've checked it out – and clocked your scene
And I've been shocked by what I've seen

Picking on those that you don't like –
So how can you really think that's right?
And hurting those that do no wrong –
How long's that been going on?

C H O R U S:
I say – hey you
What'ya gonna do?
You better watch out
'Cos I'm watching you
I say – hey you
Gotta get real
And stop and think how others feel
Give me P, E, and an A-C-E:
Peace in this community
If you don't, won't
Give it a go
I'll haunt you and I won't let go

I won't name names but you know it's you
And messing with lives is what you do
You're on my list and there you'll be –
As you don't play games with those like me

And sticks and stones they may break bones
But bones in time are mended
Yet words and names and silly games
Will always be remembered

CHORUS

Who am I? I hear you say
Well, I'm many things, in a kind of way
For I'm the voice that's in your head
And the noise at night from under your bed

I'm the banging pipe, the creaking stair
I'm everything and I'm everywhere
I'm a faceless face from the other side
Run if you like, but you'll never hide

CHORUS

Drug Rap
Valerie Bloom

We're Poppers, I'm Sugar, this is Mary Jane,
We're here to stop your heartache, here to ease your pain,
I'm Tiger, Sid, and crystal, call me Special K,
We're the drug patrol and we're here to make your day.

Don't listen, they are liars, don't check out that joint,
There's a lot of suffering sitting on that needle point,
Just stop, don't do it, that's no wonder drug,
They'll soak you in some warmth and then they'll pull
the plug.

We know right now it's hard for you to tolerate
The foolishness around you, so we'll stimulate
Your heart, your mind, your body, we will touch your soul,
Why don't you come and hang out with the drug patrol?

Don't listen, they are liars and they're up to no good,
See those broken bodies all around the neighbourhood?
A lot of people like you tried to tame the beast,
Ended beaten, sick and homeless, some of them deceased.

Say, you look a little down, we'll get you up to speed,
We'll care for you, we'll treat you right, we're all that you need,
Come on travel with us, baby, we're cool and we're hip,
And it's clear as crystal to us you could use a little trip.

Don't listen, they are liars, don't go down that track,
It's easy now to think that you will never crack,
They'll be sweetness till they have you then they'll start
   getting rough,
There are heroes made every day, but not from this stuff.

Oh, come on, don't be chicken, be one of the crowd!
Be strong, don't allow yourself to be cowed.
We'll raise your confidence and self-esteem.
A drug won't give confidence, that's just a dream.
You'll work harder with us and get better grades,
Grades drop as memory and attention fades.
We're a symbol of success, many stars are users.
Uh-uh! No-one respects a drug abuser.
Aw, c'mon, c'mon, c'mon just powder your nose.
From one little sniff a big habit grows.
But one little rock can make you feel so nice!
That one little rock could leave you cold as ice.
You can't be affected by just one little pill!
Don't gamble with your life, one dose can kill.

23

Teenage Meanage

Yvonne Mitto

Teenage
Meanage
What an age to be
I wanna be you
And you wanna be me
Fashions
Passions
Things you have to wear
Bright clothes
Right shoes
Then of course the hair
Can't be seen
To be coming off the scene
Might lose my cred
Mom sends me to bed

Teenage
Meanage
What an age to be
So much pressure
Coming from afar
Can't wait to come in late
Have my own car
Go to a bar
Stay out all night
Do things that aren't right
Have money
Jingling in my pocket
Sounds like honey
Teenage
Meanage
What an age to be

The Moon is on the Microphone (A Country Rap)

Andrew Fusek Peters

Oh the trees are dressing for an all night bop
And the sheep are going bonkers as they do the Heron Hop
And the little leaf sister
How she boogies with the breeze
As the cows do the rhythm
With the spoons on their knees.
All the birds are singin'
On Top of the Plops
And the wind he is a drumming
With a bunch of carrot tops.
The sheep are looking chic
In the latest woolly style
As they hop a happy conga
In a crocodile file
And the stars are driven down
From their mansions in the sky,
The clouds would like a dance
But they dare not even try,
So they cry-baby, hey-baby, grumble and sigh!
And the Moon is on the microphone
Crooning quite a tune
As every blade of grass
Is falling to a swoon.
Wow!
What a bop
'Til you drop
What a sight,
What a night,
What an animal rite!

Mobile Phone Rap

Brian Moses

Hi! It's me, I'm on my mobile phone,
I thought I'd give you a call to say I'm coming back home.

And I know I've got nothing important to say,
but this is my new toy and I love to play.

On my mobile phone,
my mobile phone,
wherever I go
I take my mobile phone.

Because without my phone I'm not really here,
I need a mobile phone strapped to my ear.

On the peace and quiet of a country walk,
In a crowded train I just love to talk.

On my mobile phone,
my mobile phone,
wherever I go
I take my mobile phone.

And I love to watch people watching me
and thinking how important I must be,

making so many calls and talking so much
with everybody wanting me to keep in touch

On my mobile phone,
my mobile phone,
wherever I go
I take my mobile phone.

And I'm treated real well by the phone company
they love sending all their bills to me.

Big, big bills that cost me a lot
but I don't care, I'm a real big shot

on my mobile phone,
my mobile phone,
wherever I go
I take my mobile phone.

Gran Can You Rap?

Jack Ouseby

Gran was in her chair she was taking a nap
When I tapped her on the shoulder to see if she could rap.
Gran can you rap? Can you rap? Can you Gran?
And she opened one eye and she said to me, Man,
    I'm the best rapping Gran this world's ever seen
    I'm a tip-top, slip-slap, rap-rap queen.

And she rose from her chair in the corner of the room
And she started to rap with a bim-bam-boom,
And she rolled up her eyes and she rolled round her head
And as she rolled by this is what she said,
    I'm the best rapping Gran this world's ever seen
    I'm a nip-nap, yip-yap, rap-rap queen.

Then she rapped past my dad and she rapped past my mother,
She rapped past me and my little baby brother.
She rapped her arms narrow she rapped her arms wide,
She rapped through the door and she rapped outside.
   She's the best rapping Gran this world's ever seen
   She's a drip-drop, trip-trap, rap-rap queen.

She rapped down the garden she rapped down the street,
The neighbours all cheered and they tapped their feet.
She rapped through the traffic lights as they turned red
As she rapped round the corner this is what she said,
   I'm the best rapping Gran this world's ever seen
   I'm a flip-flop, hip-hop, rap-rap queen.

She rapped down the lane she rapped up the hill,
And as she disappeard she was rapping still.
I could hear Gran's voice saying, Listen Man,
Listen to the rapping of the rap-rap Gran.
   I'm the best rapping Gran this world's ever seen
       I'm a –
          tip-top, slip-slap,
             nip-nap, yip-yap,
                hip-hop, trip-trap,
                   touch yer cap,
                      take a nap,
                         happy, happy, happy, happy,
                         rap _____ rap _____ queen.

Santa's Christmas Rapping Caper
Paul Cookson

Always the same each December
Every year since I can remember
Same old outfit, same old suits
Red and white coat, big black boots
Bobble hat and beard like snow
Ho ho boring boring Ho!

I'm sick of it, had it up to here
Same old image every year
Out with the old, in with the new
Out with the red, gimme a blue,
Orange, yellow, purple, green,
Dayglo pink, silver, cream!
Gonna check out checks, spot those spots
Deckchair stripes or polka dots

Back to front, I said back to front
Gonna wear my baseball cap
I said 1 – 2 – 3 – 4
Do the Rasta Santa Skankin' Rap
Do the Rasta Santa Skankin' Rap

Jingle bells ain't go no place
Turn up the drums, turn up the bass
BOOM! BOOM! BOOM! BOOM!
Rattle your house and shake your room
Kick that beat and let it rock
Gonna shake up all your chimney pots

Raise your roof all through the night
Christmas Eve's gonna be alright!

Back to front, I said back to front
Gonna wear my baseball cap
I said 1 – 2 – 3 – 4
Do the Rasta Santa Skankin' Rap
Do the Rasta Santa Skankin' Rap

Out with the red, in with the new
Cool and Yule and comin' for you
Gonna keep your Christmas merry
Still gonna be a cracker
Still your main man Santa
Just got a different wrapper
Love your brothers love your sisters
Live in peace not fear
I'm a Skankin' Rasta Santa
Merry Christmas! Happy New Year!

Mega Star Rap

Valerie Bloom

I'm the king of the keyboard, star of the screen,
They call me gamesmaster, you know what I mean,
'Cause I am just ace on the Nintendo action,
When I get in my stride, you know, I don't give a fraction,
With Super Mario I'm a real daredevil,
I'm cool, I'm wicked, on a different level,

I'll take on anyone who wants to challenge me,
No matter what the problem is, I hold the key,
I can tell you every short cut on the Megadrive,
I can put the Sonic Hedgehog into overdrive,
And now I would, I really would like to accept your dare,
But I've just run out of batteries for my Sega game gear.

Puss-in-footie-boots

James Carter

The tale's been told many times before
of Puss-in-Boots, so you know the score
But this one here is a brand new story
True to form, Puss takes the glory

And this here is no fairy tale cat
Or panto puss, she's where it's at
All flesh and fur, she's an actual fact
100% non-fiction cat

Now chill, relax, enjoy the match –
This brand new rap's about to hatch…

When Puss was a kit and no feet tall
Footie was her favourite thing of all
She wore her boots all night and day
And practised 'til she couldn't half play

Now once when she was down at the park
She heard a pack of hound dogs bark:
'We're one man short, so give us a shout –
if you can help the Rovers out!'

So Puss stepped up, said 'I'll have a game –
and you'll be really glad I came!'
But d'you know what? Those hound dogs howled:

A cat play footie? That ain't allowed!
As a cat can't kick – so a cat can't score
And a cat can't pass – with a little paddy paw
And a cat's too soft and a cat's too tame
So a cat can't play the big dog's game

Our heroine was not deterred,
With a Cheshire grin she softly purred:
'Boys, these sides aren't fair it seems –
I'll have to take on both your teams!'

They barked, 'We'll thrash you, pussy cat!'
'Oh yeah?' Puss laughed, 'We'll see about that!'

The whistle blew, the game began
And with that ball she ran and ran – till:
Goal number 1 – in one minute flat!
Goal number 2 – scored just like that!
Goal number 3 – a banana kick
Goal number 4 – a backward flick
For goals number 5 and 6
Puss used up more fancy tricks
She headed 7, own goal 8
So-who-do-we-appreciate?

Those dogs went crazy, angry, mad
Whatever they tried, they just looked sad
They cheated, yelled, and made a fuss
But nothing worked against our Puss

Then goal number 9 – a neat tail spin
Goal number 10 – just nudged it in
From 11 up to 21
Puss was having so much fun
The ref blew time at 24
Said ref: 'I can't watch any more!'

'Poor little pups!' Puss had to scoff
As she prepared to hurry off
But found her exit was now blocked
And then Puss had a bigger shock
Picked up, paraded 'round the grounds
And serenaded by the hounds:

She's fast she's fly she's sharp she's sweet
The niftiest feline on two feet
She's slick she's quick she's hot she's cool
And still she sticks to every rule
Watch her swing and watch her groove
You've never seen a cat like Puss here move!'
Who cares if you don't bark but miaow?
We need you on our side right now!
And sorry 'bout us lot being so mean
but will you join the Rovers' team?

'Shucks', sighed Puss, and: 'Thanks for the match,
but you guys just ain't up to scratch –
So practise loads, and then we'll see!'
With that, Puss leapt into a tree –
over the wall and down the lane
and was never seen 'round those parts again!

Haircut Rap

Valerie Bloom

Ah sey, ah want it short,
Short back an' side,
Ah tell him man, ah tell him
When ah teck him aside,
Ah sey, ah want a haircut
Ah can wear with pride,
So lef' it long on top
But short back an' side.

Ah sey try an' put a pattern
In the shorter part,
Yuh could put a skull an' crossbone,
Or an arrow through a heart,
Meck sure ah have enough hair lef'
Fe cover me wart,
Lef' a likkle pon the top,
But the res' – keep it short.

Well, bwoy, him start to cut,
An' me settle down to wait,
Him was cuttin' from seven
Till half-past eight,
Ah was startin' to get worried
Cause ah see it gettin' late,
But then him put the scissors down,
Sey, 'There yuh are, mate.'

Well, ah did see a skull an' a
Criss-cross bone or two,
But was me own skull an' bone
That was peepin' through,
Ah look jus' like a monkey
Ah did see once at the zoo,
Him sey, 'What's de matter, Tammy,
Don't yuh like the hair-do?'

Well, ah feel me heart stop beatin'
When me look pon me reflection,
Ah feel like somet'ing frizzle up
Right in me middle section,
Ah look aroun' fe somewhey
Ah could crawl into an' hide
The day ah mek me brother cut
Me hair short back an' side.

September Shoe Rap

Chris Riley

De only good ting
bout back to school
is buying new shoes
and playing de fool.

September here,
summer garn,
mi trainers off
mi new shoes on!

Mi mum say Gial
ya playin no more
keep bright, black shoe
from nine till four.

From nine till four
I sit in school,
but on mi way home
I forget de rules.

I run in de grass
kick up de dust
mi bright, black shoe
their shine don't last.

Mi mum see mi shoe,
she look real mean.
She get out the cloth
and make me clean.

I polish mi shoe
and they shine bright.
Me new, black shoes
make September all right.

The Schoolkids' Rap

John Foster

Miss was at the blackboard writing with the chalk,
When suddenly she stopped in the middle of her talk.
She snapped her fingers – snap! snap! snap!
Pay attention children and I'll teach you how to rap.

She picked up a pencil, she started to tap.
All together children, now clap! clap! clap!
Just get the rhythm, just get the beat.
Drum it with your fingers, stamp it with your feet.

That's right children, keep in time.
Now we've got the rhythm, all we need is the rhyme.
This school is cool. Miss Grace is ace.
Strut your stuff with a smile on your face.

Snap those fingers, tap those toes.
Do it like they do it on the video shows.
Flap it! Slap it! Clap! Snap! Clap!
Let's all do the schoolkids' rap!

Doin' the Rhythm of the Boneyard Rap

Wes Magee

This is the rhythm
of the boneyard rap
knuckle bones click
and hand bones clap
finger bones flick
and thigh bones slap
when you're doin' the rhythm
of the boneyard rap.
    WOOOOOOOOOOOOOOOOOO!

*It's the boneyard rap
and it's a scare.
Give your bones a shake-up
if you dare.
Rattle your teeth
and waggle your jaw
and let's do
the boneyard rap once more.*

This is the rhythm
of the boneyard rap
elbow bones clink
and backbones snap
shoulder bones chink
and toe bones tap
when you're doin' the rhythm
of the boneyard rap.
    WOOOOOOOOOOOOOOOOOO!

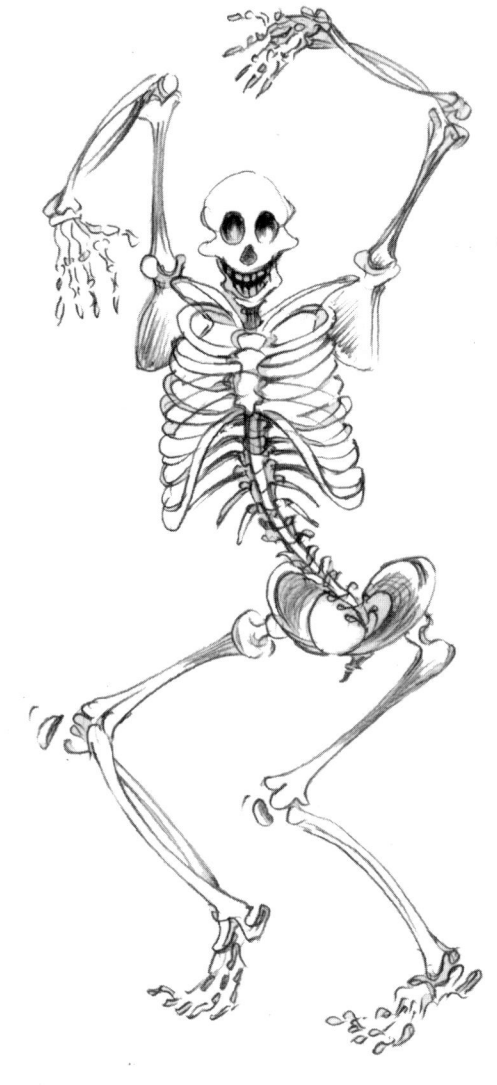

It's the boneyard rap
and it's a scare.
Give your bones a shake-up
if you dare.
Rattle your teeth
and waggle your jaw
and let's do
the boneyard rap once more.

This is the rhythm
of the boneyard rap
ankle bones sock
and arm bones flap
pelvic bones knock
and knee bones zap
when you're doin' the rhythm
of the boneyard rap.

Clapping Rap

Brian Moses

Have you ever watched how people clap,
some of them just finger tap,
some crack palms with a mighty slap,
sounding like a thunderclap.

Shy folk only clap when they know
everyone else is set in full flow,
frightened they might end up solo,
three or four claps and then it's no go!

Show-offs clap above their heads
or wave their arms about instead.
Small children clap quite naturally,
when politicians clap they actually

show the side that they support,
polite applause from the Tory sort.
Labour MPs clap as one
brothers in rhythm every one.

Some folk just go on all night,
right on left or left on right.
Some of them slice their hands like cymbals,
some of them spring them apart like pinballs.

Perhaps there should be schools that teach
proper clapping like proper speech,
keeping time or keeping pace
whatever the need or time or place.

Have you ever watched how people clap,
some of them just finger tap,
some crack palms with a mighty slap,
sounding like a thunder . . . CLAP!

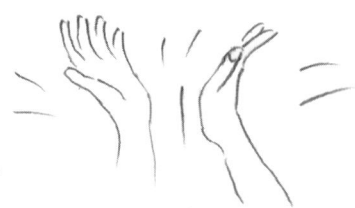

Shaggy Dog Rap

James Carter

Listen hard and listen well
to everything I've got to tell

It's not a fairy story or a scary tale
A phoney story or a pony tale

A biography or a history
A whodunnit murder mystery

A thriller, chiller – a nasty spook
A ripping yarn or a good cookbook

A sequel, prequel, West End smash
A saucy tale to make some cash

A book of a film of a radio play
of a musical of an old ballet

It's –

Well, what is it then?

I've forgotten!

Tell-Tale Rap

Gina Douthwaite

Katie Pratt's a scaredy-cat –
Wouldn't kiss Chris

 No Chris
  No Chris
   Going to tell Miss

Wouldn't hold his hand or
Let him walk her home
With Christopher Fitzdribblelip
She wouldn't be alone!

 No Chris
  No Chris
   Going to tell Miss
   Going to tell
   Going to tell . . .

Katie's in a tizz.
Katie's got her knickers
Truly in a twist
To Christopher Fitzdribblelip
All she'll say is this:

 No Chris
  No Chris
   Going to tell Miss
   Going to tell
   Going to tell . . .

But how can I resist?
Christopher Fitzdribblelip
I'll see you after six

 But don't tell
  Don't tell
   Don't tell
   Miss.

The Write a Rap Rap

Tony Mitton

Hey everybody let's write a rap
First there's a rhythm you'll need to clap
Keep that rhythm and stay in time
'Cause a rap needs rhythm and a good strong rhyme

The rhyme keeps coming in the very same place
So don't fall behind and try not to race
The rhythm keeps the rap on a regular beat
And a rhyme helps to wrap your rap up neat

'But what'll we write?' I hear you shout.
There ain't no rules for what a rap's about.
You can rap about a robber, you can rap about a king,
You can rap about a chewed up piece of string . . .
(well, you can rap about almost . . . anything!)

You can rap about the ceiling, you can rap about the floor,
You can rap about the window, write a rap on the door.
You can rap about things that are mean or pleasant
You can rap about wrapping up a Christmas present.

You can rap about a mystery hidden in a box,
You can rap about a smelly old pair of socks.
You can rap about something that's over and gone,
You can rap about something going on and on and on
And on . . .

But when you think there just ain't nothing left to say . . .
You can wrap it all up and put it away.
It's a rap. It's a rap. It's a rap rap rap rap RAP!

Madcap Rap
James Carter

Here's a little thing called **MADCAP RAP**

It's a *hippity hoppity happening* rap

It's full of `jazz` and `razzamataz`

It's got `pizzazz` like no **1** has

This rap has *feet* this rap has *style*

This rap's so *sweet* it'll make you *smile*

It'll make you *swing* like a crazy cat

It'll make you want to *BOP* and *CLAP*

Take it to the house or take it to the bridge

This rap's so COOL you could pop it in the FRIDGE

SING it, SAY it, YELL it and YAP

Let's all do the **MADCAP RAP!!**

Teachers' Manual

Using rap poems

Rap is finding its way into the classroom more and more, and via a number of routes – poetry collections and anthologies, big books for the Literacy Hour, talking book CDs and cassettes as well as workshops and live performances from visiting children's poets. One of the strengths of rap is that it is multi-faceted and has so much to offer in a classroom context. This manual aims to help teachers to exploit rap poetry to its full potential.

It would be true to say that rap poetry is not an easy form to write. It calls upon a number of resources, including:

☆ a wide vocabulary
☆ a sound knowledge of/familiarity with rhyme
☆ the ability to write within a strict rhythm(s)
☆ a knowledge of alliteration and assonance
☆ an appreciation of structure
☆ confidence and, above all, patience and perseverance

The workshops that follow are all about children developing such knowledge and skills – in terms of writing as well as performing raps. Teachers will notice that much of the workshop material is written in the second person and is aimed directly at the pupils. As a result, the material can be read aloud to or even read by classes themselves.

Some of the workshop exercises are fairly rudimentary and are aimed at helping children to develop confidence in such areas as rhythm and rhyme. These skills will need to be developed and practised either prior to or in conjunction with writing raps. However, many of the workshop activities and related worksheets on rhythm and rhyme do not necessarily have to be done in the context of rap poetry, and could quite easily be used as general poetry activities either within or outside of the literacy hour.

The current National Literacy Strategy document makes this direct reference to rap poetry:

Year 5/2 – Text Level 6: 'to understand terms which describe different types of poems, e.g. ballad, sonnet, rap, elegy, narrative poem, and to identify typical features.'

The workshops and performance section that follow cover additional requirements made by the NLS document:

Year 5/1 – Text Level 7: '. . . to consider the impact of full rhymes, half rhymes, internal rhymes and other sound patterns';

Year 5/2 Text Level 5: 'to perform poems in a variety of ways';

Year 5/3 – Text Level 4: 'to read, perform and modify a performance of poetry';

Year 5/3 – Text Level 11: 'to use performance poems as models to write and to produce poetry in polished forms through revising, redrafting and presentation';

Year 6/2 – Text Level 3: 'to recognise how poets manipulate words – for their quality of sound, e.g. rhythm, rhyme, assonance'.

Although some aspects of the workshop materials could be implemented within the Literacy Hour, teachers will observe that many of the activities would have to covered at other times.

All of the poems featured in the anthology section were written as 'rap poems' – that is, without music. On the accompanying CD there are three specially composed instrumental backing tracks to which children can perform or read pieces from the anthology or even improvise and write their own raps to. The CD also features two contemporary poets – Valerie Bloom and Brian Moses – performing their own rap poems. Suggestions on how to use the CD are given in the next section – 'Performing rap poems'.

The sections that follow – 'Performing rap poems', the photocopiable workshops sections as well as the CD – highlight the interconnectedness of language and music. They seek to help classes appreciate the musicality of poetry and to allow teachers to bring together these two aspects of the school curriculum that are only too often taught and considered separately.

The workshops focus upon such areas as the rhythm of rap poetry and actively encourage children to use metronomes and percussion instruments. Yet the material is written deliberately with the non-music-specialist in mind. Teachers should not require any prior musical knowledge, experience or expertise to use either the book or CD. Teachers can also rest assured that because rap music is such an inherent part of contemporary youth culture, children will bring to the classroom knowledge and experience of what rap is, and what it sounds and feels like and will therefore be able to contribute ideas as to how rap poetry can be used in the classroom.

Performing rap poems

Rap poetry is very much 'stage' not 'page' poetry, written with the intention that it is to be performed. To see a rap poem on a page is to see it out of context, and is akin to reading a lyric to a pop song, which can lose its value and potency when seen out of its true environment. To use another analogy, a rap poem in a book is like a musical score, lying inert, waiting to be interpreted and performed. Gaby Morgan, Editorial Director (Poetry and Non-Fiction) at Macmillan recognises this situation with regard to children's performance poetry in general:

'. . . much of the poetry we publish in our anthologies is performance poetry. And I sometimes find that as I read a piece for the first time I might respond with indifference – but when I read it out loud I'll see exactly what the appeal is, and why it works so well in performance.'

Every poet who has contributed a rap poem to the anthology section of this book will have their own way of performing their material, but these raps are open to a variety of interpretations.

The following stages should allow classes to thoroughly prepare for their own performances – in terms of a) acquainting themselves with the poems and b) exploring some of the ways that a rap can be expressed. (A summary photocopy sheet covering these issues is included at the end of the teachers' manual.)

READ IT
Children will need to read through their chosen rap a number of times to ensure that they understand each and every line. In addition, they will need to think about the tone and mood of the rap and how this can be put across in a performance. This type of work could be done by individuals, in small groups or as a whole-class activity – or a combination of these. Children can make performance notes on photocopies of the raps from the anthology.

LEARN IT
Ever seen a rapper on TV read from a lyric sheet? Of course not! To be able to give a lively and expressive performance, a class will need to learn their raps off by heart. Once children have learnt raps, they can then give time to other aspects of performance such as choreography – dancing along, clapping hands or doing gestures to emphasise certain lines, phrases or words (see 'Express It'). To help them learn their raps, children can work through some of these stages:

☆ Read the rap out loud a few times.
☆ Read the rap out loud with friends .
☆ Take the first two lines. Clap a slow beat and read the lines out loud. Then do it without the text. Do this for the whole rap.

☆ Record a reading of the poem onto audio cassette. Listen back to it a number of times.
☆ Think about the rap and recite it during a spare or quiet moment – perhaps before going to sleep or during a journey.

Less confident members of the class may need to keep a copy of the poem with them during a performance, or alternatively, one pupil could act as a prompter. Pupils tend to find it much easier to learn off by heart the raps that they have written themselves.

SHARE IT

Although rap music tends to have one rapper performing at a time, rap poetry lends itself well to being performed by a variety of ensembles:

☆ A pair could perform a stanza each and then come together for the choruses, the final verse or certain lines or phrases for emphasis. One partner could play percussion or clap or beatbox whilst the other raps.
☆ In a group, individuals could take a verse or couple of lines each; everyone could come together for the choruses, the final verse or certain lines or phrases for emphasis.
☆ A whole class could either have just a few individuals rapping the main verses or, alternatively, every class member could rap a line or two each. Again, the whole class could come together for choruses, the final verse, or certain lines or phrases for emphasis. Or, as Valerie Bloom encourages during her own rap workshops, the class could be divided into rappers, clappers and percussionists.

EXPRESS IT

As part of the choreography, facial expressions and body movements (or even dances) can be worked out to fit in with certain lines or verses.

Teachers and classes can read through their chosen rap and contribute ideas as to what body movements – with the head, hands, arms, feet and so on – could be used. Photocopy versions are useful for making notes. Also consider, if the performance will be in front of an audience, are there lines from the rap or body movements that they can join in on? If appropriate, classes could dress up as characters from the rap poems or use relevant props.

FEEL IT

It is important to consider the overall feel and the dynamics of the rap:

☆ Vary the volume, and think about which lines or verses should be quiet or soft, and which ones should be louder.
☆ Could the rap be speeded up or slowed down for certain parts?
☆ Most of all, try not to express the rap either in a monotone or alternatively, with too much enthusiasm throughout!
☆ The rhythm of the rap must be known well, and if there are any variations – such as in a chorus.

PACE IT

When children start practising their raps, they will need to take them at a slow and steady pace. Even when they become more confident they should ideally maintain the rap at this tempo. Children who begin a rap at a fast pace may well :

☆ find it hard to sustain throughout
☆ trip up on certain words
☆ run out of breath
☆ lose the meaning of the rap

Children need to be reminded prior to their performances of the importance of rapping at a reasonably slow tempo.

BEAT IT

Music, in the form of a backing rhythm, can be incorporated into a performance in a number of ways by using:

☆ PARTS OF THE BODY to create a beat – handclaps, tapping/stamping feet and beatboxing.

☆ a METRONOME. Set it to a slow beat to begin with, somewhere between 90–98 beats per minute.

☆ PERCUSSION INSTRUMENTS, for example – cow bells, cabassas, wood blocks, tambourines, shakers and hand drums. If there is a group of percussionists, ensure that the rhythm is a) quiet so that it does not drown out the words of the rap, and b) kept very simple, as a complicated rhythm will fight against the rhythm of the rap poem itself. Listen to the tracks on the CD and hear how simple and direct these are. One method of using percussion is to have it feature in certain parts of the rap, such as in the chorus, the final stanza or on certain lines or phrases for emphasis. The only way to find out what works best is to improvise and to experiment. If children are to compose a rhythm track of their own, this can be recorded onto audio cassette during rehearsals, which will enable the group to assess their performance and also help them to memorise it.

☆ THE THREE INSTRUMENTAL RAPPING TRACKS on the COMPACT DISC. It is important that children discover for themselves which track provides the most suitable backing for their chosen raps. Each track on the CD is three minutes long, so clearly, the rap to be performed can be no longer than this. The first rapping track (Track 5) is set at a slow tempo and may be useful to practise with – but this track could be used in a performance too. Some poets write rap poems in their head or even improvise them out loud – children could choose to improvise and write a rap to one of the backing tracks on the CD. For this, it is good to have pen and paper ready to jot down ideas.

MAKE IT

Classes can make their own instruments from recycled products such as plastic bottles, rubber bands, cereal packets, tissue boxes and margarine pots. Simple but effective shakers can be made with a sealed container or plastic bottle filled with dried peas, rice or old buttons. Experiment with various contents/ quantities of contents so as to produce different sounds.

GIG IT

Rap gigs have proved very popular and successful in schools. In preparation for a rap concert, classes will need to decide:

☆ whether to use raps from an anthology/their own raps or a combination
☆ how the raps will be performed (see 'Express It')
☆ whether to include clapping, percussion or a backing track (see 'Beat It')
☆ whether the raps will be performed by individuals, pairs, groups or whole classes (see 'Share It')
☆ if the audience are to join in for certain parts of the raps (see 'Express It')

Some of the raps of a similar theme from the anthology could be brought together for a rap gig, for example :

☆ raps about school : 'The Schoolkids' Rap', 'September Shoe Rap', 'I'm Watching You' and 'Tell-Tale Rap'
☆ raps about animals and the environment : 'Baby-K Rap Rhyme', 'The Charles Darwin Rap', 'Cool or Cruel?' and 'Dodo Rap'
☆ raps about fairy tales : 'Cool or Cruel?' and 'Little Red Rap' (also see Tony Mitton's fairy tale rap collection – *Big Bad Raps* - published by Orchard Books)

It is important to remember that unless the rappers are using microphones, those children doing the lead raps will need to stand reasonably close to the audience so that they can be heard.

The bonus instrumental track on the CD – track 8 – could be used as an introductory piece for a rap concert.

PLAY IT

Some raps could even be developed into a short play. Small groups could look through the anthology and discover which raps might work in this context. Consider:

☆ Would there be both speech and rap? If so, what dialogue could be included?
☆ How would the rap/play be introduced – with music or a narrator?
☆ Would the raps need to be changed – made longer or shorter, with new verses or an added chorus?
☆ Could new raps be written to perform alongside the originals?

☆ Would there be live percussion or a rhythm provided by one of the tracks on the CD or even a combination?

RECORD IT

If a school or class is going to the effort of doing a performance or concert, it is worthwhile recording it on video or audio cassette for posterity.

Recording the rehearsal stages will give instant feedback on what aspects are working well and which areas need further development.

GO FOR IT

Ever seen a shy rapper? No! Rappers need to be encouraged to really give it their all when they perform!

Writing raps workshop: rhythm

Rhythm is the most important ingredient in rap, even more essential than rhyme. If you really wanted, you could have a non-rhyming rap, but a rap without rhythm is nothing at all.

Rhythm can often be the most difficult element for young people to grasp, whether reading, writing or performing rap poems. So this is the area that needs most time and practice.

Rhythm is a word that we use most of all when talking about music, but it is just as relevant to poetry. But what is the rhythm of a poem? The rhythm depends on a number of elements, including:

☆ the words you use
☆ the sounds of those words
☆ how each word is stressed
☆ the combination of words you use
☆ the number of syllables (beats) in each word
☆ the number of syllables (beats) in each line
☆ whether you are using long vowel sounds (e.g. stay) or short vowel sounds (e.g. stop)
☆ whether the poem rhymes or not
☆ whether you are using alliteration or assonance

– but you will not need to be constantly aware of all of these things as you are writing or reading a poem. One simple way of thinking about rhythm is that it is the beat of a poem.

So, the words, the sounds of those words and the combination of the words you use are key to the rhythm of a poem. Compare the opening two lines of an early draft of the rap 'Cool or Cruel?':

You've heard a few tales about wolves like me
Saying what bad dudes we're supposed to be

with the opening two lines of the final version:

We've all heard tales of wolves like me
Telling what bad guys we're meant to be

Which opening do you think works best? Why? Think about:

☆ the rhythm and the way that the words flow
☆ the way that the words sound when spoken together

Here are a number of activities in which you can focus on rhythm in order that you can appreciate how it works in rap poetry:

☆ READ a selection of poems from the anthology in this book. For the first couple of times read them quietly to yourself, and then as you become more familiar with each poem, start to read them out loud. At first, read very slowly and emphasise the beat of each poem.

☆ LISTEN TO and READ ALONG with Valerie Bloom and Brian Moses' rap poems on the CD and concentrate on the rhythm of their poems. Tap your fingers or feet as you listen.

☆ READ some of the rap poems in the anthology aloud and to a METRONOME beat. Set the metronome to a fairly slow tempo, somewhere between 90-98. Your class can either read the poem as a whole group, or individuals can volunteer to do a verse or couple of lines each. The teacher could read the first verse to demonstrate how the rhythm is expressed.

☆ USE a METRONOME also when you are writing raps. If you don't have a metronome in your class, simply clap, tap your feet or imagine there is a slow, steady beat inside your head and write along to that.

☆ CHOOSE one rap poem from the anthology, say Tony Mitton's 'Little Red Rap'. Clap a slow, simple beat 1-2-3-4 to yourself. Say the first two lines of the poem around and around until you have the rhythm tightly fixed in your mind, and then continue clapping as you read the rest of the poem. You will find that the beats fall at these points:

CLAPS:	1	2	3	4
	Just on the edge of a deep, dark wood			
CLAPS:	1	2	3	4
	lived a girl called Little Red Riding Hood.			

When writing a rap you will need to keep the rhythm constant throughout the poem. The poet Colin Macfarlane recommends when you are writing a poem that you say the first two, three or even four lines you have written a few times over so that you know the rhythm well. This should help you to keep the rhythm steady all the way through the poem. Then try and keep those first few lines at the back of your mind as you are writing your next lines, so that the rhythm is the same. As you begin your rap, if you can't clap or tap your feet out loud, find a rhythm – a constant beat – in your mind's ear.

Some raps have a chorus. In such poems, the verses and the chorus will probably have a slightly different rhythm. Look at some of the rap poems in the anthology that have a chorus : 'Doin' the Rhythm of the Boneyard Rap', 'Cool or Cruel?', 'I'm Watching You' and 'Dodo Rap'. In each of these raps the rhythm of the chorus is different to the rhythm of the verses. Compare this verse and chorus of 'Cool or Cruel?. Read these through a few times until you know the rhythms well:

You've all heard tales of wolves like me

Telling what bad guys we're meant to be
Now I wouldn't say they're a pack of lies
But listen up close – you'll soon get wise

Hey wolfie –
Get out of town!
We don't want guys like you around
You gobble up grans, you puff little pigs
We've all had enough of your lies and tricks!

It will help you to know that there is a beat after the word 'wolfie' in the first line of the chorus. So, after you have read 'Hey Wolfie!' clap one beat and then read on from there:

CLAPS:	1		2	3	4
	Hey wolfie –			get out of town!	
CLAPS:	1		2	3 4	
	We don't want guys like you around				

The alternating verses from Norman Silver's 'New World Dream Rap' also have different rhythms:

Can you hear the celebration
spreading all around the nation?
Like a flaming supernova
love is breaking out all over.

Do you see the warning
written on the sky?
Come another morning
it may be you or I.

On your fingers count the number of syllables (beats) there are in each line of any of the raps in this book. You will find that each line in a rap poem has approximately the same number of syllables.

Should you find that the rhythm doesn't sound right or seem to flow when you are writing your own rap, try:

☆ counting the beats per line
☆ adding more words/phrases if they are needed
☆ changing the words/phrases you already have
☆ shortening the lines by removing words/phrases
☆ re-writing the whole line (or even verse) – and saying the same thing but by using different words

Try not to think too much about the beats as you are writing your first draft. Concentrate on getting your ideas down, and during your second draft you can go back and see if the rhythm is right, and if you have too many or too few beats in each line. The following worksheet, 'Rhythm – Syllables', will help you to get into the habit of counting syllables.

You should be able to hear if the rhythm of your rap poem is working as you read it to yourself. If you are ever in any doubt, ask a friend to read the rap out loud to you, and then you will hear if the rhythm is right.

R H Y T H M
SYLLABLES

photocopy sheet

Think of words for each of the syllable numbers below. It may help to count the number of beats on your fingers.

Word	Syllables			
	1	**2**	**3**	**4**
Town/City	*York*	*Bristol*	*Manchester*	*Greater London*
Girl's Name	*Ann*			
Boy's Name		*Simon*		
Food			*Broccoli*	
Drink	*Tea*			
Animal			*Stick Insect*	
Sport		*Swimming*		
Musical instrument				*Synthesiser*
Number		*Eleven*		

Here is the first line from Valerie Bloom's 'Mega Star Rap', divided into its syllables:

> I'm/ the/ king/ of/ the/ key/board,/ star/ of/ the/ screen/ (11 syllables)

Now divide up the next three lines to 'Mega Star Rap' and count the syllables:

> They call me gamesmaster, you know what I mean
> 'Cause I am just ace on the Nintendo action
> When I get in my stride, you know, I don't give a fraction

Writing raps workshop: rhyme

Alongside rhythm, rhyme is what helps provide the music of a rap poem. Two other elements – assonance and alliteration – also play important roles, but first we'll look at rhyme.

What is rhyme? Put simply, rhyming words are those that fall at the end of a line in a poem and have the same sound :

> Just on the edge of a deep, dark *wood*
> Lived a girl called Little Red Riding *Hood*
>
> ('Little Red Rap' – Tony Mitton)

There is a lot to think about when writing a rap – such as telling a story, keeping to the rhythm and of course, finding good rhymes. An acceptable short cut is to use HALF-RHYMES. (See worksheet 'Rhymes & Half-Rhymes' that follows.) Sometimes people use a word in a rap poem simply because it rhymes, even if it doesn't quite make sense. A half-rhyme is a much better alternative, as Tony Mitton suggests:

'I'm not strict about rhymes – half-rhymes such as 'rap' and 'Jack' are fine, or even assonant sounds are good – like 'pass' and 'fast'.'

Look at these lines from rap poems that have half-rhymes:

> With 'him' and 'thing' -
>
> As everyone thinks I'm just like him
> But I don't scare folks – it's not my thing
>
> (from 'Cool or Cruel?')
>
> With 'tough' and 'luck' -
>
> Survival – you got to be tough
> Survival – or is it luck?
>
> (from 'The Charles Darwin Rap')

Rhymes not only depend on the sounds of the words, but also the number of syllables:

> ONE SYLLABLE: boy/toy, coast/ghost, build/drilled
> TWO SYLLABLE: heaven/seven, bigger/digger, drying/frying
> THREE SYLLABLE: perfecting/reflecting, history/mystery, December/remember

– however, triple-syllable rhyming words tend not to be as common as single and double rhymes in rap or any form of poetry.

There are different ways of using rhyme in poems. These are called RHYME SCHEMES. Have a look at the rhymes in this verse from the poem 'The Walrus and the Carpenter' by Lewis Carroll:

> The sun was shining on the sea (A)
> Shining with all his might (B)
> He did his very best to make (C)
> The billows smooth and bright – (B)
> And this was odd because it was (D)
> The middle of the night. (B)

The rhyme scheme is ABCBDB.

Work out the rhyme scheme for this verse from the poem, *A-Sitting on a Gate*, also by Lewis Carroll:

> I'll tell thee everything I can;
> There's little to relate.
> I saw an aged aged man,
> A-sitting on a gate.
> "Who are you aged man?" I said.
> "And how is it you live?"
> And his answer trickled through my head
> Like water through a sieve.

Rap poems tend to stick to a rhyme scheme of AABBCC, as in the opening verse of Jack Ouseby's rap poem 'Gran Can You Rap?':

> Gran was in her chair she was taking a nap (A)
> When I tapped her on the shoulder to see if she could rap. (A)
> Gran can you rap? Can you rap? Can you Gran? (B)
> And she opened one eye and she said to me, Man, (B)
> I'm the best rapping Gran this world's ever seen (C)
> I'm a tip-top, slip-slap, rap-rap queen. (C)

When rhymes come at the end of every two lines like this, the lines are known as RHYMING COUPLETS.

If you are writing a rap poem and you are looking for a rhyme, there are a number of things you can do:

☆ Say the word at end of your last line is 'log'. Either in your head or on paper you could go through the alphabet putting each letter in front of 'og' to find a suitable rhyme. With the first six letters of the alphabet you would end up with the following – 'aog', 'bog', 'cog', 'dog', 'eog' and 'fog'. Two of these words – 'aog' and 'eog' – don't exist, so you would have to ignore these. [See worksheet 'Rhyming Alphabet' that follows.] You may also find that the rhyming words you end up with are either a) spelt quite differently, for example – 'shoe'/'grew', 'high'/'sky'; or b) have a different number of syllables, as in these lines:

So gather up close, take a seat, *relax*
and check these out – my radical *raps*

(from 'Cool or Cruel?')

A book of a film of a radio *play*
of a musical of an old *ballet*

(from 'Shaggy Dog Rap')

☆ Use a half-rhyme. So for 'dig' you may choose 'pin', for 'cat' you may use 'lap' or for 'new' you may choose 'group'.

☆ Go back to your previous line and think of different ways of finishing that line, with either a different word or a different phrase that will make it easier for you to find a rhyme in the next line. Or you may find that you need to change the whole of the previous line. Make a list of all the words/phrases you come up with. You could even use a thesaurus to help you find alternatives.

☆ Go to a rhyming dictionary. This should be your last choice, as it is good to practise your rhyming skills.

ASSONANCE and ALLITERATION are closely related to rhyme and are often used in raps. (See worksheets 'Assonance' and 'Alliteration'.)

ASSONANCE occurs when words contain the same sounds, but during a line, for example:

'How *far* is the *car*?'
'Is this *my tie*?'

As with rhymes, assonant words can have very different spellings:

'Where did that *crow go*?'
'I need *four more*.'

ALLITERATION occurs when when words begin with the same sounds:

'We wish.'
'Short, sharp, shock.'
'Talk to Tom.'

Look for ALLITERATION and ASSONANCE in these lines:

The sheep are looking chic
In the latest woolly style
As they hop a happy conga
In a crocodile file

('The Moon is on the Microphone' – Andrew Fusek Peters)

Look for ASSONANCE in these lines:

> Katie Pratt's a scaredy-cat
> Wouldn't kiss Chris

('Tell-Tale Rap' – Gina Douthwaite)

> This school is cool. Miss Grace is ace.
> Strut your stuff with a smile on your face.

(The Schoolkids' Rap – John Foster)

GENERAL TIPS ON RHYMING

☆ Work hard on finding good rhymes; try not to give up too easily.

☆ Use the Rhyming Alphabet sheet (or make one of your own on scrap paper).

☆ Remember that rhymes may sound similar but may look different – take 'grew'/ 'shoe' or 'high'/'sky'

☆ Try not to use a word just because it rhymes; if it doesn't make sense in your rap poem, then it doesn't belong!

☆ Don't be afraid to use half-rhymes; a half-rhyme that makes sense in your rap is better than a rhyme that doesn't make sense.

☆ If you're really stuck for a rhyme, why not ask someone else if they can think of a rhyme for your word?

☆ Use a rhyming dictionary – but only if you have to!

RHYME EXERCISES:

NONSENSE POEMS: Tony Mitton encourages young poets to practise using rhyme by writing nonsense poems. Take a word such as 'cat'. Think of all the rhymes for 'cat'. Make a list of them. Now write a nonsense poem, in which you use as many 'cat' rhymes as you can. For this exercise, your poem doesn't have to make any sense at all – and you can even use a rhyming dictionary to help you find plenty of rhymes. Other words you could use are 'ball', 'cake' and 'hair' or you could think of your own.

'DOWN BEHIND THE DUSTBIN': Another rhyming activity Tony Mitton suggests is to take Michael Rosen's poem 'Down Behind the Dustbin', and to write your own verses. Again, it doesn't matter if the verses don't quite make sense, this exercise is just a practice. You can find this poem in either *You Tell Me* (with Roger McGough – Puffin) or *Wouldn't You Like to Know* (Scholastic).

RHYMING ALPHABET

photocopy sheet

Write the word that you want to rhyme with here:

....

Now slowly go down the alphabet below, putting the sound of your word after each letter/string of letters. For example, if your word is 'show', you would get 'a-ow', 'b-ow', 'bl-ow', br-ow', 'c-ow', 'ch-ow', 'cl-ow', 'cr-ow' and so on.

A	N
B	O
Bl	P
Br	Pl
C	Pr
Ch	Q
Cl	R
Cr	S
D	Sh
Dr	Sl
E	Sm
F	Sn
Fl	St
Fr	Str
G	Sw
Gh	T
Gl	Th
Gr	Tr
H	U
I	V
J	W
K	X
L	Y
M	Z

RHYMES & HALF-RHYMES

photocopy sheet

Think of rhymes and half-rhymes for the words below.

Word	rhyme	half-rhyme
CAT	PAT	LAP
TREE	ME	FEEL
THROUGH		
BUY		
SINK		
WEIGH		
KNOW		
NEAR		
NOW		
SHINE		
DEEP		
POND		
SAIL		
PET		
HOT		
SHUT		

ASSONANCE

photocopy sheet

Assonance is when words close together have the same sound.

Note how in this sentence there are many words that sound the same but are spelt differently.

Example: Sue too knew who threw the new shoe in the zoo.

Write your own fun sentences with the words below and using as much assonance as you can. Don't worry if your sentences don't quite make sense!

FOUND:

VIEW:

WAY:

BRIGHT:

SING:

MOON:

ALLITERATION

photocopy sheet

Alliteration is when words close together begin with the same sounds. This example is quite a tongue-twister:

Brainy Brenda brought brilliant Brian some broken brown bricks.

Write your own fun sentences using as much alliteration as you can. Not all of the words that you use have to have the same sound, for example, 'So Tom took his time.' And don't worry if your sentences don't quite make sense!

RED:

COLD:

FIVE:

BUBBLE:

GRASS:

LID:

CREEP:

MANY:

SNOW:

photocopy sheet

Writing raps workshop: theme

The THEME is the subject of the rap poem, be it –

   ☆ A STORY – as in 'Little Red Rap', 'Cool or Cruel?', 'September Shoe
     Rap', 'Puss-in-Footie-Boots'

   ☆ A MESSAGE – as in 'I'm Watching You', 'New World Dream Rap',
     'Baby-K Rap Rhyme', 'Drug Rap', 'Dodo Rap', 'I De Rap Guy', 'The
     Write a Rap Rap'

   ☆ A COMIC SITUATION – as in 'Haircut Rap', 'Gran Can You Rap?',
     'Schoolkids' Rap', 'The Moon is on the Microphone', 'Tell-Tale Rap'

   ☆ A BIOGRAPHY (or autoiography) – as in 'I De Rap Guy', 'The Charles
     Darwin Rap'

Some rap poems can have more than one theme. For example, Benjamin
Zephaniah's 'I De Rap Guy' is an autobiographical rap that also has a serious
message; likewise, 'Baby-K Rap Rhyme' is a comic rap with a message.

When you are thinking about writing a rap poem, find a theme or a subject
that interests you or choose from one of the workshop ideas that follow. The
list of what you can write about in a rap – as Tony Mitton says in his 'Write a
Rap Rap' – is absolutely endless!

Theme workshops

TELLING A STORY: FICTION

Telling a story – a story that you have to invent yourself – is one of the most difficult things to do in a rap. It is easier to re-tell a story that already exists – as Tony Mitton has in 'Little Red Rap'. This is called a RE-TELLING.

Choose a well-known fairy tale, such as:

☆ Sleeping Beauty
☆ Snow White
☆ Rapunzel
☆ The Story of the Three Little Pigs
☆ Hansel & Gretel
☆ Tom Thumb
☆ Puss-in-Boots
☆ Cinderella
☆ Aladdin
☆ Rumpelstiltskin
☆ Beauty and the Beast
☆ Goldilocks and the Three Bears

– or a book, either modern or traditional, such as:

☆ Lewis Carroll's *Alice in Wonderland*
☆ Ted Hughes' *The Iron Man*
☆ a *Goosebumps* or *Point Horror*
☆ a Jacqueline Wilson novel
☆ a Terry Pratchett novel
☆ *The Demon Headmaster* by Gillian Cross
☆ a Roald Dahl book such as *James and the Giant Peach* or *Fantastic Mr. Fox*
☆ one of JK Rowling's *Harry Potter* books

Most importantly, choose something that you have enjoyed reading. Once you have chosen, write down the plot – the events of the story – in a few sentences to make sure you can remember it. If you read through 'Little Red Rap' you will notice that Tony Mitton has not included all of the details from the original fairy tale. Similarly, you may choose to only tell of the main events and characters from the story in your own rap.

Decide if you are going to tell the story in the traditional form, in the third person – writing about events using 'he'/'she'/the characters' names – as in 'Little Red Rap' or, in the first person, so that one of the characters tells the story – as in 'Cool or Cruel?'. When a character tells the story in this way – in the first person – it is called a monologue.

Examples of fairy-tale monologues would be a rap in which Jack told the story of *Jack and the Beanstalk*, the Beast telling the story of *Beauty and the Beast* or one of the pigs telling *The Story of the Three Little Pigs*.

If you were to choose a Jacqueline Wilson novel such as *The Story of Tracy Beaker*, you could write a rap in the voice of Tracy, or if you chose a *Harry*

Potter book, your rap could be in the voice of Harry.

You could even mix and match fairy-tale characters together, such as:

> What if the giant from the beanstalk turned up at Cinderella's ball?
> What if Jack swapped his cow for Aladdin's lamp and not some seeds?
> What if the witch from Hansel & Gretel turned up as Goldilocks was eating the bears' porridge?

This is the beginning to eight-year-old Megan Campbell's merging together of 'Hansel & Gretel' and 'Little Red Riding Hood':

> Once upon a time in fairy tale land
> lived Hansel and Gretel who just couldn't stand
> Their stepmother who left them in the wood
> and there they met Red Riding Hood . . .

'Cool or Cruel?' is a brand new tale, based around the son of the Big Bad Wolf from *Little Red Riding Hood*. You could do this too. Think about fairy tales that you know and see if there is any material for a new story, such as:

> What happened to the ugly sisters after Cinderella married?
> What if the witch in 'Hansel & Gretel' survived? Who would she taunt next?
> What if the prince turned back into a frog?

– or, you could adapt and modernise a traditional fairy tale, such as *Rapunzel*, *Bluebeard* or *The Story of the Three Little Pigs*. Note that *Rapunzel* even begins with the word 'rap'! Patience Agbabi has written a *Rapunzel* rap – called 'RAPunzel' – why not write your own?

If you are telling or re-telling a fairy tale you may want to create a beginning of your own or use/adapt one of these:

> Once, in a land so far away . . .
> Once upon a time there lived a . . .
> A long time ago in a faraway land . . .
> Once there lived . . .
> This is the tale/story of . . .

Any story at all can be told in the form of a rap poem, from Shakespeare's play of *Romeo & Juliet*, to Bible stories, to Disney films and even soap operas such as *Neighbours* or *EastEnders*!

However, you may decide that you want to invent your own story and tell it in a rap poem. Or, you may already have a story written out that you want to turn into a rap. If you are going to invent a story from scratch, it will help if you write down the plot or main events of the story first – either in a few sentences or in a flow diagram.

TELLING A STORY: NON-FICTION

Just because you are telling a story does not mean that you have to stick to fiction. 'The Charles Darwin Rap' is a rap re-telling of a science book written over 150 years ago.

Science is a rich source of non-fiction material for raps, with subjects such as:

☆ The planets, stars, the solar system and space travel
☆ Electricity
☆ The body
☆ Food chains
☆ Animals and the natural world, including minibeasts
☆ The miniature world of atoms and molecules
☆ New inventions

If you are interested in history, you could write a rap about:

☆ an historical figure – Henry VIII, William Shakespeare, Cleopatra, Elizabeth I, Joan of Arc
☆ an historical event – the Roman invasion, the Battle of Hastings, the moon landing, the Gunpowder Plot, the building of the Egyptian pyramids or Stonehenge
☆ an historical period – Romans, Tudors, Victorians, World War II, the 1960s, the 19th century – or even pre-history, such as the time of the dinosaurs

Another aspect of non-fiction is geography. Perhaps you live in an interesting village, town or community. This rap was written by Year 6 pupils at Bangabandhu School, in Bethnal Green, London, with poet Valerie Bloom in a rap workshop:

Bethnal Green Rap

Halfway round the Central Line
Jump off when you see the sign
Bethnal Green's the place to be
For a taste of history.

Check the air raid shelter down the tube
Take your ration book, you might get some food
As you walk in through the door
See that mattress on the floor?
Grandad's comfort in the war,
We don't need that anymore.

Upstairs to the library –
D'you know what it used to be?
Listen to those moans and screams
Patients living tortured dreams
Through the bars daylight gleams
Illuminating nightmare scenes.

Watch their lives as people go
Down cobbled streets in the peepshow:
Dolls in corsets and frilly frocks,
Men in tights instead of socks,
White long johns and petticoats,
Collars tight around men's throats.

The Museum's fun but it's time to eat,
Shall we check out Nando's on Wilmot Street?
I'd like some chips from KFC.
Deep Pan Pizza's the place for me.
KFC? McDonald's? No!
Café Alba's the place to go.

Halfway round the Central Line
Jump off when you see the sign
Bethnal Green's the place to be
For a taste of history.

(Written by Year 6 pupils with Valerie Bloom
at Bangabandhu School, Bethnal Green, London)

A MESSAGE

Some rap poems have a message to put across. Three of the raps in the anthology talk about aspects of the environment – 'Baby-K Rap Rhyme', 'I De Rap Guy' and 'Dodo Rap'. Another rap tells of world peace, namely Norman Silver's 'New World Dream Rap'. The theme to the rap 'I'm Watching You' is bullying in schools. Valerie Bloom's 'Drug Rap' is all about the harmful effects of taking drugs. In Tony Mitton's 'Write A Rap Rap', the message encourages people to write their own raps.

There are many messages that you could put across in your own rap, and here are a few suggestions:

☆ Endangered animals
☆ The environment
☆ Homelessness
☆ Racial harmony
☆ War
☆ Caring for people
☆ Bullying

You may well have a theme of your own, perhaps something that you feel strongly about.

The key here is to *show* and not *tell*. Try not to *tell* people that 'violence is bad' or 'bullying is wrong', instead, *show* people through your words the reasons why something is wrong and actually *show* the effects of violence, bullying, pollution or whatever.

In your rap you could ask questions. You could ask why people do the things that they do. Read through some of the raps mentioned above and see how these raps get their messages across. A chorus is useful for a rap with a message as it gives your readers or audience something to join in on and it will make the rap more memorable.

In Valerie Bloom's 'Drug Rap' there are two voices. Why not write your own rap in which there are two different voices discussing/debating a subject? This type of 'duologue' rap would lend itself to being written by a pair.

Some raps can be humorous but can still make an important point. 'Cool or Cruel?' is a fun rap but it has two underlying messages: one is that you must not judge people by appearances or by what others have said; the other is that wolves are not actually the dangerous animals that fairy tales have portrayed them to be. Write your own rap, as with 'Cool or Cruel?' or 'Dodo Rap' – in the voice of an animal, perhaps an animal that has been mistreated or misunderstood.

You could write your own functional rap, such as:

☆ an ansaphone rap
☆ a rap to welcome people to a website
☆ a rap to advertise a product on TV or on the radio
☆ a rap to advertise a forthcoming event – a school play, football match or a concert
☆ a rap to wish someone a happy birthday
☆ a rap to celebrate a special event

A COMIC SITUATION

Read through Wes Magee's 'Doin' the Rhythm of the Boneyard Rap'. Do you know any local ghost or horror stories? Is there a house near you that is meant to be haunted? Write your own fun ghost or horror story rap. Give it a catchy chorus.

'Haircut Rap' tells of a comic domestic situation. Think of something that has happened to you or members of your family, and tell the story in a rap in your own voice. Or, why not tell about your family from one of your pets' points of view?

'The Moon is on the Microphone' tells of the community of the natural world having a dance. Think of other natural world communities in books or films. For instance, have you seen the Disney films *A Bug's Life* or *The Jungle Book*? You could tell these stories as a rap. There can also be a community of toys. Think of the Pixar/Disney film *Toy Story*. You could write a rap from Woody's point of view about his rival, Buzz Lightyear.

A MONOLOGUE OR AUTO/BIOGRAPHY

Benjamin Zephaniah's definition of rap – 'a rhythmical monologue' – also neatly describes a number of raps in the anthology, which are themselves monologues, raps told by a single character.

In some of these raps, the person telling the rap – the 'narrator' – tells of their life or they give their opinions on life or tell of their world view, as in 'Baby-K Rap Rhyme' and 'I De Rap Guy'. Another biographical rap is 'The Michael Rosen Rap' by Michael Rosen, which can be found in his collection *The Hypnotiser*.

In your monologue rap you could tell the story of:

    ☆ yourself
    ☆ someone that you know
    ☆ a famous person
    ☆ a fictional character – someone from a film or a book

If you are writing in the voice of another person, give thought to the way that person speaks and the type of language that they use.

If you are writing a monologue about your own life, then you could use this introduction or write one of your own:

    Hey everybody, listen to me!
    This is my biography!
    My name is . . .

SHAPE UP

'Madcap Rap' in the anthology is not just a rap, and a nonsense rap at that, but also a shape poem. Certain words in the poem have been made into various shapes - see the words 'bridge', 'swing' and 'smile' for example. Other words have special fonts to bring out the meaning of that word, such as 'cool', 'fridge' and 'style'. You could either write your own shape poem rap from scratch, or you could even write your own lines to 'Madcap Rap'. As with 'Madcap Rap', your rap doesn't have to make sense, it too can be full of nonsense! You can either work on a computer or write/draw your rap by hand.

FREE CHOICE

Perhaps you have a favourite subject, hobby or a topic that interests you. Before you begin your rap, brainstorm some ideas. Find some aspect of your subject that you could write about. Say that your interest is football. You could write about your favourite team or player or a particular match you have watched.

These two rap poems were free choice :

Laurence Fitz-Desorgher (aged 9) is interested in bats, and his rap is about a vampire:

    Count Rapula

    So you've heard the story about Count Drac
    But I want you to forget about that
    This here is about Count Rap –
    ever so cool with his backwards cap!

    His ghetto blaster in his hand
    Listening to his favourite band
    His favourite rock band is called Korn

And he looks real cool with his jeans all torn!

Alasdair Fitz-Desorgher (age 11) wrote about one of his favourite subjects too :

Artist Rap

Yo, I'm the artist who lives 'round here
Yeah, I paint pictures of far and near
I paint all day and I paint all night
And my paintings always turn out right

The colours range from pink to green
The wildest colours you've ever seen
The paints make sounds a bit like this –
Listen up there's quite a list :

Splish
Splosh
Splitt
Splodge
Squidge
Splidge
Splott
Splatt . . .
How's that?

Here are some suggestions for topics :

☆ Life in the year 3000
☆ A recent news item
☆ Your three wishes
☆ Fashion
☆ Your school or class
☆ Life in the playground
☆ Brother and sister
☆ An alien's view of earth

General tips on writing rap poems

☆ Brainstorm your ideas first. Quickly write down any words, phrases or lines that come to you.

☆ If you are improvising a rap to music or writing a rap in your head, keep pen and paper handy so you can jot down your ideas.

☆ Chant your first few lines over a few times in your head to make sure you know the rhythm of your rap well.

☆ Write your rap to a fairly slow but steady beat.

☆ You will need to do a few drafts of your rap poem. In the first draft, don't worry too much about the rhythm or the rhymes, concentrate on getting down all the ideas that come to you. In your second or third draft you can improve the poem by working on the rhythm and the rhymes and the overall flow of the rap.

☆ It is generally better to write rap poems by hand than on the computer. Once you have done your first full draft, you could then type it out onto a PC. Next, do a printout and develop the rap further from there. When you have a final draft you could experiment with different fonts and sizes for your words.

☆ Raps are often written in dialect, for example a Caribbean dialect; see 'September Shoe Rap', 'Haircut Rap' and 'I De Rap Guy' for examples. What part of the United Kingdom do you come from? If you speak in a certain dialect, you could use the language of your dialect in your rap. Otherwise, use the language that you use every day.

☆ Here is a list of points you might want to consider when drafting your rap:

Do you repeat some words too often?
Do all your rhymes work well?
Are you using some words just for the sake of a rhyme?

How does the rap sound when read aloud?
Is the rhythm working well?
Listen hard to the rhythm of each line – does each line flow?
Do you keep to the same rhythm?
Does your rap need a chorus?

Do you have a good beginning, middle and end?
Does the opening grab your attention and make you want to go on?

Are your lines the right length?
Do you have roughly the same number of syllables in each line?

If you have gone through these points and you are not sure what needs to be done next, leave your rap poem for a while and come back to it later.

She's hip, she's fly, she's cool, she's street
This puss can pass . . . . . —
put in 1st person?

Puss-in-footie-boots (rap)

The tale's been told many times before
of Puss-in-Boots, so you know the score
But this one here is a brand new story
True to form, Puss takes the glory
So Chill, relax, enjoy the match —
This brand new rap's about to hatch...

Now ~~T~~his here is no ~~fairy~~ tale cat
Or panto puss, I'm where it's at
All ~~I'm~~ flesh and fur, ~~I'm~~ a feline fact
~~As I'm an actual factual cat~~
And so's the tale that I tell now
Here it comes to you right meow!

Once when she
~~Ever since I~~ was no feet tall
I'd always wanted to play football -

EITHER : And once when I was sat on a wall
I saw a sight that nearly made me fall
For over in the park, as I recall
A bunch of hounds were kicking a ball
And when their ball came flying my way
I had to duck to get out of its way

OR : I went to the park every Saturday
To watch those hound dogs play and play
Then once the thought just came to me -
Why were there no cats in the team?
So once when a side was one dog down
Puss here offered to help them out
And d'you know what? Those hound dogs howled :

A cat play footie? That ain't allowed!
As a cat can't kick - so a cat can't score
And a cat can't pass - with a little paddy paw
And a cat's too soft and a cat's too tame
So a cat can't play the big dog's game

This cat's got attitude.
cat's got style }?
100% non-fiction cat

fast asleep
on top of a wall
The wall was the
edge of a big green park

Suddenly Puss
heard a bark
. . . .

AS A RESPONSE TO THIS ?

Goal #1 . . . .
Goal #2 . . . .

☆ Share your rap with a friend or a group and give each other positive feedback.

On the page opposite is an early and incomplete draft of 'Puss-in-Footie-Boots' by James Carter.

Compare this with the final version. What are the main differences?

What is rap?

R A P
  I S
    A
     W A Y
      O F
       T A L K I N G

A R A P P O E M has 3 main ingredients:

R H Y T H M

R H Y M E

T H E M E

A R A P P O E M:

☆ has a strong RHYTHM

☆ uses RHYME

☆ has a THEME – which is either a STORY
   or a MESSAGE

☆ often has the word 'RAP' in the title

☆ uses everyday, COLLOQUIAL language

☆ is often written in a DIALECT, such as a
   Caribbean dialect

How do YOU describe rap?

Responses from JUNIOR CLASSES – Years 4, 5 and 6:

'fast rhymes'

'the rhythm has a strong beat'

'it's a poem that rhymes'

'it's all on one note'

'quick-speaking like in the Spice Girls'

'mainly all drums..not many instruments'

'nearly every line has the same amount of words'

Responses from POETS:

Valerie Bloom:
'Traditionally, rap was a tool for expressing discontent with the system. It was a voice for protest that used heavy rhythmic patterns.'

John Foster:
'A rap's a kind of poem
With a steady rhythmic beat
Full of rhymes and wordplay
That'll make you tap your feet.'

Brian Moses:
'Words spoken fast over a beat.'

Benjamin Zephaniah:
'A rap is a rhythmical monologue.'

A history of RAP and RAP POETRY

RAP has a long history – one that can be traced back to 'TOASTING' in Jamaica (talking over reggae records) and before that to the poetry of 'GRIOTS' (musicians-storytellers) in Africa.

RAP – in its modern form – comes from a type of music called HIP-HOP.

HIP-HOP is a Black American music that began in the early 1970s in the city of New York in America.

HIP-HOP has a strong RHYTHM and uses SAMPLES and BEATS from other songs.

HIP-HOP has become the most popular type of music in America.

The best known AMERICAN RAPPERS today include LAURYN HILL and WILL SMITH.

Now RAP can be heard in many different types of music – such as POP and ROCK and DANCE – and many other places, such as cartoons and films and music for adverts on TV.

Throughout the 1980s and 1990s, POETS in both America and Britain began to write their own form of raps – RAP POEMS without music.

RAP POETRY is one of the most popular forms of POETRY for young people.

Performing rap poems

READ IT

Read the rap many times so that you understand each and every line. Think about the tone and mood of the rap and how you could express this in a performance.

LEARN IT

Ever seen a rapper on TV read from a lyric sheet? If you want to give a lively, exciting performance you will need to learn your rap off by heart.

SHARE IT

Why not perform a rap with others – a friend, group or even the whole class?

EXPRESS IT

You can use facial expressions and body movements to fit in with certain lines. Or, you could find a suitable costume or use props.

FEEL IT

Think about the overall feel and dynamics of the rap. Vary the volume and speed where appropriate. Try not to say your rap a) in a monotone or b) with too much enthusiasm.

PACE IT

Always remember to take your rap at a slow and steady pace.

BEAT IT

All kinds of different things can give you a backing rhythm: handclaps, tapping/ stamping your feet, beatboxing, a metronome or percussion instruments.

MAKE IT

Why not make your own instruments from recycled products?

GIG IT

Why not do a rap gig at your school? Choose some of your favourite rap poems or write your own.

PLAY IT

Why not adapt a rap into a short play?

RECORD IT

If you are going to the effort of doing a performance or concert, record it onto video or cassette.

GO FOR IT

Ever seen a shy rapper? Of course not!

A rap glossary

A L L I T E R A T I O N – words close together that begin with the same letters or sounds : 'We wish', 'Talk to Tom'

A S S O N A N C E – words close together that have the same sounds : 'Where did that *crow go*?', 'I need *four more*'

B A C K I N G   T R A C K – a piece of music to sing or rap along to

B E A T B O X – making a drum machine sound with your mouth and using your hands as a sound box

C H O R U S – a catchy verse repeated a number of times throughout a poem, rap or song

C O L L O Q U I A L   L A N G U A G E – everyday language

D I A L E C T – the language of a specific place, for example, the Afro-Caribbean dialects or the Geordie dialect of Newcastle

H A L F - R H Y M E – when words at the end of a line have the similar sounds :

People think that I'm just like *him*
But I don't scare folks, it's not my *thing*

H I P   H O P – a musical form that comes from New York; hip hop has a strong rhythm and often uses samples from other songs

M E T R O N O M E – an instrument that helps musicians play to a steady beat

M O N O L O G U E – a story or speech performed by one person

N A R R A T O R – a person that tells a story

R H Y M E – when words at the end of a line have the same sounds :

Now once when she was down at the *park*
She heard a pack of hound dogs *bark*

R H Y T H M – the beat of a poem, song or piece of music

S Y L L A B L E (also known as a B E A T) – a single beat in a word; 'fish' has one syllable' – 'happy' has two syllables

T H E M E – the main subject of a poem, story, song, film or play

V E R S E – (also known as a STANZA) – a group of lines in a poem